Getting Rich Is Glorious: Chinese Secrets to Business and Money

by Angelina Zhang

Book 2 of the "China Insider Guide" series by Angelina Zhang

I0476440

Getting Rich Is Glorius

China is rich, kind of

China is rich now. If you watched the news in the US, or even in China, you'd come to that conclusion. Any media mention of China is full of mentions of record-breaking sales of private jets, Rolexes, Ferraris, and hundred-million-dollar mansions at the personal level, or of Chinese companies buying up everything in sight at the corporate level. If you live in a tourist destination in the Western world (or, in fact, anywhere), you would think that China is a nation of $100-bill-carrying, free-spending, Louis-Vuitton-buying obsessive tourists and shoppers.

Indeed, China's GDP, corporate profits, and average living standards have been rising quickly for the past thirty or so years. Now only 7% of people in China live on under a dollar a day, which is a common benchmark value for third-world poverty. And the purchasing power and sheer impact of Chinese consumers and companies worldwide is undeniable.

Yet the story isn't that simple, because while only 7% of China lives on less than a dollar a day, about 70% of china lives on less than five dollars a day. (Statistics from World Bank.) That's total income, for housing, food, medicine, everything. Less than $150 a month. And there's not much of a social safety net in China, as we'll discuss, so there are no government assistance programs to add to that $150 a month. Since 2012, most people in China live in cities, but if you saw the living conditions of the average city-dweller in China, they're not much different from rural poverty: dirt floor, hole-in-the-ground bathroom, a bowl of rice once a day, and so on.

Much of the "wealth" accumulated in China in the past ten years is illusory: it's based on "tulip mania" type value increases in the value of real estate and Chinese stocks. Until recently, Chinese people were formally only allowed to invest in real estate, nothing else (although informally the truth was much different) -- this led to real estate becoming like casino chips, and empty condo buildings standing around China. How can real estate prices in both rural and urban China be about the same as in the United States, when people's salaries are about 90% lower in China? And to "diversify," Chinese people nowadays invest in stocks, leading to a big runup in share prices over the past few years, and a lot of "wealth" creation -- but almost all this stock-purchasing is based on symbols on screens and whispered "hot stock tips," with most retail investors having not even the slightest idea of fundamental stock value or analysis.

Despite that illusory recent wealth, which I'm not too focused on here, China does have a history of business and economic strength, and of building tremendously successful and profitable businesses and families -- even absent recent bubble markets and Communist Party money-grabs. This book seeks to explain why China and Chinese people are successful with money and business, and how you can use this knowledge to your own advantage, whether as an example of what to do, as an example of what *not* to do (as might be true for some Chinese business behaviors I consider unethical), or as a guide for what your Chinese clients, suppliers, or employees are thinking.

That China's economic power has been steadily rising in the past thirty years is undeniable. But China didn't start thirty years ago with economic liberalization or ninety years ago with the founding of the Chinese Communist Party. China is four thousand years old. China invented much of what we consider to be modern capitalism. Depending on which historian you believe, ancient China invented all or some of these bulwarks of modern business and capitalism: cash, coins, interest-bearing loans, corporations, and securitized business risk. China has always been into money, and for thousands of years, China was a world leader in commerce and industry.

So China's recent economic rise isn't the case of a dark-horse unknown suddenly appearing, perhaps as a one-hit wonder of economic development, the way, say, the nation of Nauru had a meteoric rise and fall in the 1980s. Instead, China's rise is a return to China's usual position of being an economic powerhouse. Business is an integral part of Chinese culture, even more so than more commonly known cultural icons such as dragons or chopsticks. Chinese people can easily imagine China without dragons (not such a huge deal inside China actually) or without chopsticks (which were more or less illegal during the most hardline communist years), but Chinese people can't imagine China without business. From the smallest street ice-cream vendor to the biggest state-backed manufacturing tycoon, every Chinese person, every Chinese family, every Chinese house, every Chinese social institution, is filled with concerns of money and business.

What are China's unique beliefs and practices having to do with money? Why has China been such an economic powerhouse for much of its history? Indeed, why do Chinese people tend to do well in business even when they go far from China? Well, my own career in banking is a small, funny example of "Chinese business success abroad," but consider that

Chinese people have a strong, perhaps dominant presence in the business environments of every place from Los Angeles to New York to Buenos Aires to London to Lagos to Bombay to Bangkok to Manila to Sydney to Auckland -- research the business community of any of those cities, or of similar cities anywhere in the world, and you will find a very strong Chinese business presence.

As I first traveled by car around the United States some ten years ago, around the most "backwater" parts of the country, I continued to be reminded of this fact, as I found successful Chinese business people in the most unlikely places. Of course, upon seeing an Asian, maybe even recognizably Chinese, in those "unlikely places," the Chinese people in question usually approached me, so perhaps I saw them more clearly than a non-Asian might have. I still remember the furniture merchant whose ancestors were from Chaozhou who spotted me in a rural one-stoplight town in southern Illinois. And the restaurant-owning family, descendants of the Taishanese people who built the railroads, whom I met in a desert town alongside I-80 in Nevada. And so on. Those are only the most unlikely-sounding American examples. Look in "more likely" places, such as, say, the surnames of small business owners in New York or Los Angeles, and you are likely to be hit in the face with a wall of Chens and Changs and Lis and, yes, Zhangs. Chinese-Americans have net worths and incomes that are among the highest in the United States, generally higher than those of the Anglo-Americans who had a few hundred years ahead of them in getting started in American business.

So, anywhere in the world, for Chinese people, there's got to be something special in the water. Some cultural practices or attitudes have to be contributing to Chinese people's being universal, for four thousand years, so good at money and business. What parts of it can you study and learn, perhaps only to better understand our money culture better, or perhaps to take something of Chinese money culture for yourself, or perhaps to be better at doing business with or even against Chinese people?

I'm not going to tell you to become Chinese and start doing just as this book says. I'm not presenting Chinese people's ways as a model for you to emulate it. Whether you want to emulate the Chinese way, or merely study it, or maybe throw it away with revulsion, is up to you. There's no one right way to live and no one right way to manage your money and business, contrary to what self-help books may tell you. And so I'm not going to force or even cajole you to adopt the Chinese ways, because maybe they're not for you. Many of them are not even for me. But you can't decide for yourself unless you understand those practices.

I'm going to take you inside the Chinese mind and the Chinese business, and describe everyday life and attitudes, as an insider, but an insider who has lived in the US long enough to know what parts of those attitudes are remarkable or noteworthy for an outside observer. Most importantly, I will go beyond the usual cliches of "China is very big," "Chinese people like to work hard," and "China is communist but omg it's so capitalist." You can save those kinds of impressions or analyses for a tourist's blog, because that's about as good as they are.

Can I cover all of China's one billion people and all of China's four thousand years of history in this little book? Probably not. But I promise that this book will give you an excellent foundational understanding of the Chinese mindset and culture of money and business.

Let's get started.

Our mind on our money, our money on our mind

You're a Chinese person, in China, in 2015. You feel chest pain and go to a public hospital. What do you think is the first thing you'll be asked at the emergency room? Your medical history? The nature of the chest pains? No. You'll be asked to pay a cash deposit, or secure a written payment guarantee from your insurance company. Don't have enough insurance or cash for the proposed treatment? You'll be physically carried outside the hospital and placed outside on the street and told not to come back. Even if you have some but not all of the money. Even if you're in the middle of a heart attack. Even if you promise you'll be able to pay the bill later. Even if you're very young, or very old, or very handicapped. You're unlikely to find any sympathy from people on the street. You might be arrested for blocking the sidewalk. In jail you won't get any medical treatment either.

Welcome to "capitalism with Chinese characteristics," as it's called by the Chinese government. The official story is that Chinese capitalism is humanitarian, well-tempered, and focused on social harmony. That's something no one in China believes -- certainly none of the Communist Party talking heads believe it, not any more than they believe the other fairy tales they tell. We Chinese people know the reality of "capitalism with Chinese characteristics," and it is focused on material gain, single-mindedly, and to the exclusion of everything else. That's nothing new. It's not invented by the current Chinese economic reformers, nor even by their fathers or mentors. It's been part of

China longer than most likely any reader of this book has been alive.

In China, and in Chinese culture, you are your cash. Your entire value to navigate the world around you is related to your cash -- maybe with some allowance made for your illiquid assets (businesses, real estate) and your intangible assets (government connections). Have you ever watched the movie Glengarry Glen Ross? There's the famous speech in the movie that goes: "I made $970,000 last year. How much did you make? You see pal, that's who I am, and you're nothing. Nice guy? I don't give a shit. Good father? Fuck you! Go home and play with your kids." To Chinese people seeing that movie character, there's nothing remarkable or unusual to what he's saying -- with perhaps the modification that in the Chinese mindview, a poor person cannot be a good parent.

Does this sound like a dystopian science fiction novel? Or like some kind of Ayn Rand fantasy? Well, it's China, today and for much of its history. Through and through. Your money is your value in life and in the world. Everything from your treatment in an emergency room to your child's grades at school to your access to the legal system is determined by your wealth.

And in China, no one does anything for you for free, unless they have some kind of pre-existing relationship with you or they explicitly owe you a favor. Lose your wallet? The finder will demand a ransom that you can negotiate with them for the wallet itself and the documents and cards in it, and it's understood that they will keep any cash in that wallet. Need directions on the street? No one wants to be bothered, unless you offer them cash to help you. And so on and so on.

My boyfriend in New York once came upon a very lost Chinese couple walking around Williamsburg, Brooklyn. They were on vacation from China, and were trying to get to an art gallery they had read about that was showing some Chinese art. My boyfriend took out a sketch pad and drew them a map to where they needed to go, and walked them some of the way there. They were not pleased or impressed but shocked and scared -- for what kind of fee he would expect for the service. They were shocked during the walk over, and my then-boyfriend was equally shocked when he handed them the drawn map and bade them on their way and they took out a wad of cash and asked him "what is the price?" Their likely final impression of my boyfriend, who turned down their money, as any average American would do? Probably not "nice guy helping a stranger" but "insane guy going around working for free."

Admittedly, mainland China is at the extreme end of this sort of attitude. I do think that in part the attitude comes from ancient Chinese culture, even earlier than communism, but I also think that it's been encouraged and abetted by communism. This money-or-nothing attitude is much less pronounced in Chinese communities free of Chinese communism, such as Taiwan, Hong Kong, and Singapore, as well as Chinese communities in the Western world. The average person in those societies still holds money as very important, more likely more important than a person in the Western first world, but is much less likely to believe that it's perfectly just for someone who can't afford to pay for medical treatment to die on the street.

So imagine being mainland Chinese and knowing that your access to pretty much everything in life depends on how much money you have. Even if you weren't inclined to be a very materialistic person, wouldn't you become one? If you knew that, for example, your child will be allowed to die on the street if you can't pay for her medical treatment, or starve on the street if you can't afford to pay for her food, wouldn't you start caring a lot about how much money you can accumulate? This makes China's materialistic culture self-sustaining and self-perpetuating. If your whole world only cares about cash, then you'd better have enough cash, or else you die.

If you visit a doctor in China, the doctor will see you as nothing more than a profit opportunity. That is a simple factual statement. For Americans, that would be a cynical, pessimistic view about the medical (or any) profession, and someone who expressed that view of a doctor would be accused of perhaps only assuming the worst about people. In China, everyone knows that the doctor only wants to make money from you. No one would expect anything else from a doctor. The doctor will give you effective treatment only insofar as it helps his business interests -- for example, because you will live longer and be his customer, or because you will recommend that other people visit him. That is all you can hope for. In Chinese culture, a doctor who lets concern for your well-being override his financial interests would be considered at worst insane, at best eccentric and quixotic -- in any case, a highly unusual sort of person.

What would a first-worlder say about such a doctor? A first-worlder might say such a doctor is highly unethical, maybe even immoral or evil. But when this doctor, living in China, knows that his own access to healthcare, his own family life, his own ability to obtain schooling for his kids or police protection for his family, depends only on how much cash he has -- can you fault him for caring only about cash?

If you visit a judge or a police officer or a teacher or other "public servant" in China, it's almost certain that all they will interested in will not be helping you but financially helping themselves. That is an accepted part of Chinese life, and is also why immigrants from China are so distrustful of public officials in their newly adopted countries. But how much can you blame these "corrupt" government officials? If, again, everything in their whole life is determined by how much cash they have and how much cash they can pay for whatever? If their official salary is, say, $500 a month, and to keep their kids in school and keep their wives happy, they need at least $5,000 a month, which is how much each of their colleagues is making from "unreported income" -- what in the world else are they supposed to do? As I wrote in my earlier book, *Chinese Girl Confessions*, in Chinese culture, it's normal to choose your boyfriend or husband depending on how much money he has or is willing to give you, and perfectly normal to leave that boyfriend or husband when a better monetary opportunity comes along (although there is a big penalty in market value for divorced women, so divorce will happen only if the new opportunity is much better than the old one). So not measuring up in terms of wealth can affect not only your access to basic public services, but also your access to a spouse, very drastically and directly.

Have you seen how much young Chinese women these days dress up, wear makeup, style their hair, and sculpt their bodies (through exercise or surgery or both)? They're not doing that for fun. They're doing that because being physically attractive is their only route to cash, through having either a rich husband or at least a sugar daddy. If you asked an American woman who likes to dress up why she's always dressed up, and she told you, "to find a rich man," you'd guess she was joking. If a Chinese woman told you that, she would be stating bland, accepted reality, not anything unusual or funny.

Given all that: doesn't it make sense that Chinese people are interested in making money? And these facts instantly brand as seriously misguided any romantic notions of Chinese people being non-materialistic, whether you believe so because of some kind of romantic idea of Chinamen riding around on rickshaws and painting lotus blossoms, or because of a similarly romantic idea that communism makes people uninterested in money. And the economic growth and historical economic strength of China is not by sheer luck, but, among other reasons, because Chinese people think about money nonstop. Always. Without a break.

Have you ever heard the theory that, for example, Mozart was a great composer and Picasso was a great painter primarily not because of "natural talent" but simply because of how much time they were able to devote to pursuing their goals? Part of Chinese people's success with money has to do with simply how focused they are on it, in all aspects of their lives.

Choosing a religion? Choosing a spouse? Choosing a hobby? Planning your children's futures? Planning what to eat for dinner? For each of those decisions, a Chinese person's primary, and perhaps only, consideration would be the financial benefits of the decision.

This may seem especially extreme when applied to religion. You may have heard about the growth of Christianity in China. What you may not have heard is that typical Chinese Christians know or care very little about Christian theology, but are attracted to Christianity as it's seen as the religion for rich people -- and associating oneself with Christians will make the right business connections, and will also bring good financial fortunes upon oneself. In a reversal of American stereotypes about who goes to church, in China, Christian churches are a place for well-off people. Most Christian churches in China would indirectly or even directly turn away poor people; their poverty might rub off on fellow churchgoers, and ruin the "successful" atmosphere of the church. (If you are a Christian who is offended by this, please don't kill the messenger. I'm only telling you the truth about China. I didn't create Chinese culture.)

In regards to choosing a spouse, the financial aspect is as important for men choosing women as it is for women choosing women. And those are the only options, as gay marriage is considered an unthinkable abomination in China.

You probably know, or can guess, that money is a Chinese woman's primary consideration in choosing a spouse. But it's also a Chinese man's very important consideration when choosing a woman. Directly choosing a rich woman is culturally acceptable only if the woman's economic level is no higher than the man's own economic level. If a man wants a woman no poorer than he is, that is fine, although most women in China want a man who has at least twice the woman's level of income and wealth. If a man wants a woman who is richer than he is, he is derided as a "soft rice man," kind of a ponce or a sissy. A man who "eats soft rice," sometimes called a "soft rice king," is financially supported by his wife. What is far more common than being a "soft rice king" is looking for a woman who the man thinks will be helpful or compatible with his own financial goals. This is ascertained by analyzing the woman's background and demeanor, her father's financial status, and, importantly for this form of fortune-telling, her face and other physical features: certain physical features on a woman, such as a big forehead, are associated with being conducive to the husband getting rich. In fact, it's a bit of a parlor game (although taken seriously) in Chinese circles, and on the Chinese internet, to analyze the physical features of Chinese bigshots' wives, to try to gather their "secrets of success."

Hoping to get rich from your spouse's forehead is too superstitious for my tastes, but I've been corrupted by life in America. To an average Chinese person, there's nothing silly about that idea. I don't believe in the forehead thing, but I do believe that we Chinese people are on to something. Your choice of life partner or spouse is in fact the most important choice you will make to affect your long-term financial well-being. Foreheads or not, it's obvious to me that a spouse can indeed make you rich or poor. And while the Chinese 100% focus on the financial aspects of a potential spouse might be excessive (of course, my "100%" figure it itself a bit of exaggeration; maybe 95% is more realistic), I also consider excessive the Western romantic ideal that tells us never, ever to think about the financial implications of a love interest. Unless you don't care about how rich or poor you'll end up -- and that is fine, if that is indeed your preference -- I think it's useful for Westerners to learn something from Chinese culture, and think beyond good looks, even beyond current bank balances, and think about how someone will contribute to your financial situation in the very long run.

To my mind, and even to the Chinese mind, that financial consideration includes a lot of things, many of which overlap with the usual Western romantic considerations. For example, is your potential romantic interest someone who demands that you never stay late at work, and be home every day at 6 P.M.? To a Chinese person, that would be a huge red flag that this person won't be conducive to your wealth accumulation. To a Westerner, that would be a huge red flag that this person is controlling. Same result. Be careful about that person.

The financial considerations can be more subtle. Social climbing through dating and marriage are universal. In China, such arrangements go to almost comical extremes. As a very real example, consider the story of the car mechanic who my parents in Shanghai go to: his wife married him because her parents wanted to start a car rental business, and those parents limited her marriage options to either a car mechanic or a bank loan officer. In America, parents would say this jokingly, but Chinese parents lay these out as very real requirements. Bank loan officers were socioeconomically a bit out of reach for this woman, so she found a car mechanic to marry -- and her new husband did indeed help his parents-in-law with their new car rental business, and they are now well-off thanks to the arrangement.

As another example, when I was a university student in China, I received a marriage proposal from the son of my parents' friends, to whom I had only spoken online a few times. We had chatted online in a friendly manner and gotten along fine, and one day he proposed that we should marry. Why? Because my family is from the Hongkou neighborhood of Shanghai, and his family wanted to invest in real estate in Hongkou. That's it. That's why he thought we'd make a good husband and wife. When I was hesitant about this -- maybe I'd already absorbed some foreign thinking even before leaving

China -- he assured me that he was quite certain our families could make a lot of money together.

Not that marriages for family power are foreign to the Western world. Until romantic ideals took over the Western world only a few hundred years ago, Westerners, especially rich Westerners, also married for family business connections. Famously, royal families married to maximize power and territory. So don't rant about Chinese people being inhuman. Anachronistic, maybe, but not quite inhuman, because all cultures used to do this. Just that Chinese culture got more into it than the others, and never quite got out of it.

But for Chinese people, it's not just marriage partners or religions that have to do with financial considerations. Everyone knows the famous Chinese parental preference for sons over daughters. That is, of course, financially based, as in the Chinese mindset a daughter has less income potential than a son, and may place her husband's and parents-in-law's financial interests above her own parents' interests. It goes much farther than that. People try to conceive their baby at times of the year that are especially "wealth-bringing"; that is why there is a baby boom in China during dragon years and years ending in the number 8 (a wealth-bringing lucky number in Chinese superstition), and also why disproportionately many Chinese babies, including me, are born around Chinese New Year.

Buying and decorating a house? A primary concern for Chinese people is the house's placement in regard to natural features such as mountains and rivers, so as not to "block the flow of wealth" into the house. And when the house is being designed, perhaps the most important feature of the house is a design that "keeps wealth in" and "doesn't let wealth run out" --

sort of a superstitious version of Western considerations of energy efficiency.

And so on and so on. Every seemingly minuscule personal decision is evaluated according to how it will affect a person's wealth. Many of the criteria are superstitious and mythological. I don't believe in them, but I must tell you that many highly financially successful people in China absolutely believe in these superstitions, and openly attribute much of their success to reasons I (and probably you) would consider silly mythology.

But here is my explanation of this: even if having a house with a doorway that doesn't let wealth out doesn't actually do anything, the knowledge and confidence that you have this type of house may have the effect of a self-fulfilling prophecy. Someone who believes that they checked all the boxes and are well prepared (through superstition) to make a lot of money may in fact work harder, be more open to opportunities, be more confident in their decisionmaking, whatever. Call it psychosomatic effects, or the power of self-esteem, or a self-fulfilling prophecy, or whatever, but it does seem to have a strong effect. Don't Westerners do much the same thing, with the culture of "daily affirmations" and self esteem boosting? I think that in Chinese culture, assuring yourself that all the mythological forces are lined up to make you rich has the same effect as "daily affirmations" have in Western culture. I don't have a journal citation for you. I don't know if any respected psychologist or anthropologist has ever proposed this theory. It's only my theory. But it makes a lot of sense to me.

In addition to giving us affirmations and self-esteem, the constant focus on how everything relates to our financial well-being also creates financial discipline, or a money obsession, depending on your perspective. Have you ever heard of the Buddhist training that teaches you to always be aware of your breathing, so that you remember whether you were inhaling or exhaling when you woke up? The Chinese culture of thinking about finances even when you see your potential spouse's forehead also means that Chinese people are very aware of finances when they actually are handling money, even in small amounts. There is an Asian-American stereotype about older Chinese people fiercely fighting over a penny. That is very much true. To Chinese people, money, in any amount, in any context, is so important that it's never wrong to worry about. Have you heard the famous (and true) fact that when China's government executes someone, they make the family pay for cost of the bullets? That is just another form of the Chinese context that in no context -- not even an execution -- is it wrong to count your pennies.

If you want to get rich, counting your pennies is the way to go. That's indisputable. And that probably has a lot to do with Chinese people's great degree of success in money and business. Only you can decide for yourself whether it's worth it. As I warned you, this book isn't going to push you to become Chinese. I, personally, think that the Chinese attitude to money isn't worth it to me. I would have more money if I constantly pestered my boyfriend for expensive gifts I could resell, or if I demanded a refund every time a restaurant meal didn't taste so great, or if I followed several Chinese friends' advice to save on a Starbucks latte by ordering an Americano and then pouring free milk into it. It is indisputable however that having this degree of minuscule control over every penny you spend, your money always on your mind and your mind always on your money, is going to help you become rich. Whether it's worth it is up to you.

Inside, outside, relationships, and opposite poles of trust

Imagine a filthy concrete apartment building, unpainted and unmaintained for decades, with garbage and human waste often thrown out its doors if not its windows. Inside that building, individual family living spaces are immaculately maintained, obsessively cleaned, with no expense spared. You might think I'm relating a metaphor, but this is literally how a typical Chinese middle-class dwelling looks. In addition to being literal reality, it's also a good metaphor for the all-important Chinese distinction of "inside and outside." Chinese people, perhaps more so than any other cultural group, make a tremendous, diametrical distinction between "inside" and "outside." You can see this in those apartment buildings, or in a typical Chinese car driver who keeps his car immaculate but doesn't hesitate to throw trash out the window as he drives,

A common observation foreign visitors make about Chinese society is that people do anything and everything for close friends or relatives, but would never help a stranger. In the Western world, it would be very odd to ask your friend to lend you money to buy a house. In Chinese society, that's the essence of friendship. That also means that you can only trust your friends not to cheat you, and don't trust strangers.

Sociologists study something called "in-group preference," and compare different cultures in terms of their relative degrees of "in-group preference." It's a popular concept for MBA students to learn. The basic idea is: how much better will you treat, or how much more will you like or trust, a close friend, as opposed to a stranger? First-world Western societies are always said to have the lowest degrees of in-group preferences. The ideas of "treat all people equally" and "kindness to strangers" have real resonance and authority in the minds of, say, Americans, Germans, and Britons. On the other hand, East Asian societies, especially Chinese societies, are notoriously very, very high in terms of in-group preference.

Unscientifically, I would say that mainland China has probably the world's highest degree of in-group preference. You can see this in the common observation from visitors to China: "Chinese people are so nice to friends, but so terrible to strangers." That's a common observation. A Chinese person would respond to that: "well, of *course*! What else would you expect?!" Perhaps it's because historically, China was an agrarian society in which everyone stayed in his respective village (in which everyone is extended family anyway), and outsiders were assumed to be robbers. Perhaps because Chinese culture, or at least its Confucian form, emphasizes fulfilling your functional obligations in regards to your relationships with people -- usually familial relationships, literally or metaphorically -- and there is no category for how to treat strangers, other than the recommendation to be wary of them, because they are people who have no obligation toward you.

In China, it is common to make mental or even photographic or written note of the serial number of a currency bill you hand someone for payment in a shop or restaurant -- because if you don't, that person is likely to swap it for a fake, and tell you that you gave them that fake. In China, watches that require servicing are considered undesirable, because no one would trust a repairman with their watch: usually such a repairman would swap the inside mechanism for a broken one and claim your watch is broken. At a mobile phone repair facility in China, customers demand to stand watch over the technician (often facilitated with a window specifically for this purpose), to make sure that the technician doesn't surreptitiously swap their iphone for a fake. There's a saying: "In a Chinese market, only the buyer and the seller are real." (Meaning: everything else, including the seller's goods and the buyer's money, is fake.)

On the other hand, in China, it's not uncommon to ask a close friend or family member to replace you at work for a few days, or to help you move, or, most importantly, to lend you money. While consumer lending is not well-established in China -- buying apartments, houses, and cars on bank credit is not unheard of, but is not too popular -- informal family-and-friends credit is everywhere. If someone in China calls you their friend, it shouldn't be surprising if they ask you to contribute to a loan for their house or car purchase, and you can expect the same from them. Do these informal credit arrangements sometimes go bad? Sure. But unlike the case with a formal credit report from a bank, informal bad credit can't be rebuilt, at least not in one lifetime. And considering how crucial friends are in a society with such extreme in-group preference (where you trust your friends almost totally ,but strangers not at all), the repercussions of losing your credibility with friends are severe. Unlike the case in the US, you can't expect strangers, social organizations, or the government to help you in bad times. All you have is friends and family. (And that is also why sons are so important to Chinese parents: they are the Chinese equivalent of social security or pensions.)

In America, people are taught not to mix business with pleasure, not to lend or borrow money with friends, and generally to avoid employment or business relationships with friends. To a Chinese person, that is entirely backwards. In a society where you can't trust strangers, Chinese people have a very strong preference for restricting business and employment only to friends and relatives. "Mixing business and friendship" is the only way to survive in the Chinese mindset, because if you do business with strangers, you'll be ruined by it. If you want to hire someone to work the cash register at your shop, it has to be a close friend or relative, because it's assumed that a stranger will cheat you. If you want to have your iphone fixed, you either go to a friend's or relative's shop, or literally stand guard over your phone as it's being fixed, or you can assume that your good phone will be surreptitiously swapped for a broken or fake phone.

An American employer is usually made uncomfortable by the prospect of hiring friends or relatives. A Chinese employer would be similarly uncomfortable hiring strangers. Although on the surface these attitudes may appear to be completely opposite, there is some similarity, because when the level of trust desired is really extreme, even Americans prefer to work with friends and family. As an MBA, I'm thinking here of famous startup entrepreneurs -- Google, Facebook, whatever -- almost always started by a small team of best friends, or sometimes relatives. Donning my organizational-analysis glasses, that's probably because in a highly fluid organization, contracts and formal systems of trust don't go far enough to protect what you think is right -- maybe you'd trust a stranger cooking in your restaurant, but you wouldn't trust them with your billion-dollar social network idea. So maybe from a certain angle, American and Chinese attitudes aren't so different. But to the most casual observation, this does mean that you may be surprised by the "lack of boundaries" or "nepotism" in a Chinese business.

If you meet a Chinese business owner and then are introduced to his (almost always *his*) immediate underlings, almost all of them will be relatives. When Chinese people meet other Chinese people, they proudly announce that the vice president is their brother, the technical manager is their uncle, the salesperson is their nephew, and so on. This demonstrates that we are all closely connected and work as a team, and our organization has its house in order. It's as important as it would be important in the West to show people's years of experience or educational credentials. But there might be some self-censoring when such business people meet a Westerner, as Chinese people nowadays know that the Western world tends to frown upon "nepotism" in business staffing. If you are introduced to a boss's assistants and underlings, try to look at their noses or ears or mouths or whatever your favorite method of ascertaining shared ancestry -- because in any business but the most large-scale and impersonal company, the management will be mostly related to one another.

What's the advantage of this? The big advantage is obvious when you remember that China doesn't have a well-developed system of civil law and corporate regulation, nor of credit rating and formal reputation tacking. In first-world countries, if an employee cheats you, you can sue them, or in some cases, report them to law enforcement for prosecution; in China, any government intervention into such matters is haphazard, may take years, and has results largely based on bribes. One way to enforce trust in such an environment is the method you see in movies: the Chinese mafia. Yes, there is mafia in many forms in China. But the other way to enforce trust, less violent and perhaps less movie-worthy, is by having only relatives and close friends working with you. And why exactly would they not cheat you? Because if you're their friend and relative, you are also crucial to their survival. In a world where strangers can't be trusted, maintaining good relations with friends and relatives is key.

People with even a cursory understanding of China know about the concept of "guanxi," or relationship. You can call it social capital or connections. "Guanxi" is the extent to which you are considered an "insider" or a "friend" in people's social networks. The raw, guanxi-less world is a vicious place, where strangers will never help you. But if you have lots of guanxi, everyone around is your friend. In a first-world society where trust is enforced by credit bureaus, regulatory agencies, liability insurance companies, and civil courts, relationships are still important -- but not to the extent that in China, your relationships, your social capital, your "guanxi," entirely determine your success.

If you study a rags-to-riches story in China -- I mean study its reality, not the official story that might be altered to fit foreigners' moral tastes or the Communist Party's propaganda goals -- you will find that the only way to go from rags to riches in China is to successfully manage your guanxi. You become something like a horse-trader with personal relationships. There's a similar concept in the Western world: a power broker. But a power broker is someone who can get things done, often in a very impersonal way, just by making deals between powerful interests. Chinese guanxi is much more personal than that. An American rags-to-riches story most often features someone who is either very smart or very hard-working. Seldom does a rags-to-riches story involve someone who had the right connections. In China, however, a fierce work ethic is perhaps something everyone has, so there's not much chance of distinguishing yourself there. And as for being brilliantly smart -- there is value placed on the right university attendance and so on, but it is only a fraction of the value placed on social connections, or guanxi.

Suppose you somehow dropped out of the sky and landed in China as a rich business owner or government official or executive in China. Suppose, because we are imagining you just dropped out of the sky, you have this position of yours, and you have a lot of money and a lot of smarts and an amazing work ethic, but you don't have any relationships to count on. You don't have any guanxi. You're not too social or maybe you just haven't had time to cultivate relationships or maybe for whatever reason people just don't like you. Well -- if you are such a person in China, you won't keep your wealth for long, unless you plan on hiding your money in a vault you will always guard. If you don't have any guanxi, everyone around you will shave a few zeroes off of whatever they owe you, and moreover, you won't be able to get anything done.

Keep in mind, also, that guanxi is always a matter of competing loyalties. Anyone older than an infant has a complex network of guanxi relationships, and they are often competing with one another. Your close friend who is your boss asks for you to work salary-free for one month, but your mother wants you to buy her a new car that month -- and so on and so on. And the people around you also have competing guanxi loyalties. That means that if they don't have any guanxi to you, they will act on the guanxi they have to other people. So if your company accountant has no guanxi with you, he will steal money from your company to protect his guanxi with his brother who needs an operation, or will give your customer a ridiculously low price to protect his guanxi with the purchasing manager who might hire him in the future. Your guanxi is never in a vacuum. That's why you hire *close* friends or relatives for key positions: you only hope that your company purchasing manager has more alliance to you, his *first* cousin, than he has to the vendor's salesman who is his *third* cousin! It's an interesting business landscape when courts, lawyers, and law enforcers, not to mention strangers, cannot be trusted upon to provide security and trust.

And guanxi is always the property of the individual, and not the job position or the company. This is why traditionally Chinese businesses are strongly associated with an individual owner. Most successful Chinese companies are strongly based on one man (almost always a man), and that man is the owner and the boss of the enterprise; the idea of separated management and ownership never quite reached Chinese thinking. This is also why many Chinese companies are simply a form of the owner's name or family name. They benefit from the guanxi of that name and that person; a business not associated with a person's personal guanxi would have a big uphill battle. In fact, such a business usually hires someone in the community who has a lot of guanxi with intended customers and other key contacts.

Unlike the case with merchants and fellow community members, or even individual government officials, the government itself as a whole holds no guanxi with anyone. The government is seen as something we called a "roving bandit" in my MBA economics classes -- basically a roving mafia that extorts payments from you, doesn't do anything useful, and, importantly, does as it wishes, without any control from you (China never was a democratic society!). So if you are an accountant, will you help your boss, with whom you have strong guanxi, or will you help the tax authorities, with whom you have zero guanxi? It sounds simplistic, but that is what it comes down to. And what the Western world might call corruption or even a culture of crime, we Chinese people just call keeping our loyalties in order. Actually, that kind of attitude is not so uncommon in America's worst ghettos, where law enforcements is seen as an evil outside force, and you only have your guanxi relationships to live by: you will probably help your relatives and fellow gang members, rather than the "roving bandit" that is the police.

I once brought up the song "I Get By With A Little Help From My Friends" in an MBA class in the US, when discussing Chinese attitudes to guanxi and connections. That song is quite popular among Chinese people of my generation -- yes, the Beatles are still now youth culture in China, the way they were decades ago in the rest of the world, presumably because few of our parents or grandparents listened to the Beatles when they were new, so they never became uncool. Anyway. That song really perfectly fits the only way to succeed in China: with a little help from your friends. (Oh, also that day I found out from my American classmates that the song is actually about drugs --

well, I can assure you that in China we took the song's lyrics at simplest face value, and that's how I'll continue to remember it in my mind!)

What can you stand to learn from this for your own financial and business life? Well, if you plan on doing business in China, the answer is extremely obvious, and I don't think you need me to tell you: doing business in China means building and managing guanxi relationships. Of course. That's more basic than knowing not to stand your chopsticks in a bowl of rice. But what can you glean from the Chinese concept of inside-outside if you are thousands of miles from China, and just want to do things better in your own world, perhaps in the US?

My answer would be that you should consider the advantages of not keeping the solid, impenetrable, quintuple-barbed-wire-protected barrier Americans often have between business and friendship. "Don't do business with friends or relatives" is a well-known American maxim, and I guess the Chinese equivalent is "Don't do business without friends or relatives." The reasons and arguments may be less obvious, when you do have a legal system to count on, and when Americans tend to be generally honest and trustworthy even toward strangers.

The flip side of that is that the Chinese attitude is that you shouldn't express trust or kindness to strangers. Chinese people think it's ludicrous -- or at best oddly quixotic -- that Westerners donate to charity or anonymously help other people. There's no denying it: you will financially be better off individually if you never donate to charity and never help someone unless you expect them to help you back. Is it worth it? That's something only you can decide. What I can advise you is that when you wonder how those rich Chinese people got so very rich, you understand that part of it meant never "wasting" their money on anonymous charity, and instead "investing" their money with friends and family who will also help them.

That goes back to the cultural belief in always having our material well-being on our minds. Even when Chinese people give or help, it's seen as an investment. A parent funds a child's education only because that child is expected to later financially support that parent. This is also why Chinese parents are infamous for neglecting or even abusing children who are handicapped, or not academically high-achieving, or, in the old days, female -- because any investment in those children will not pay off.

And Chinese immigrants in the US? Well, "it depends." With limited access to formal credit and formal law enforcement, of course recent Chinese immigrants initially fall back upon the system of depending on friends for everything from borrowing money to dealing with the police. Almost any Chinatown, or even any area of the US with Chinese immigrants, will have several Chinese business lending institutions or "borrowing clubs," called "hui" in Chinese, where the members pay monthly dues and are then allowed to borrow from the common money pot as they gain credibility in the community. The trust system depends on deep connections of friendship and family; your lender is not just someone in an office, but also may be your cousin, who is also your brother-in-law, who is also your accountant, who is also your kids' Chinese calligraphy teacher.

Maybe to some extent, Americans nowadays have few friends. In the United States, you're likely not to even know your neighbors' names -- never mind the idea of borrowing money from your neighbors! But when Chinese people see Americans who have tremendous social networks but don't use them for financial or business gain, they see that as a tremendous resource lying idle and never used. In the Chinese mindset, it's a resource not only unused because Americans usually don't, say, borrow money from their friends, but also because Americans don't often use their personal networks to contravene government regulations or laws. Sure, that happens sometimes, but not to the universal extent it would in China. I remember when I was telling some of my relatives in China that I have to pay a lot of income taxes (especially living in New York) -- and they were amazed that despite my having known my boss for several years, and despite him actually being ethnically Chinese, he and I had never conspired to have me work "off the books" tax-free and thereby almost double my income. "Is it because you and he don't like or trust each other?" my relatives asked. And of course, no, it's not. But "let's do some crime, my friend" is not the first thing on Americans' minds in a friendship. Or at least not in mainstream America.

And the advice from this for your own money management? Your friendship networks are indeed a valuable business resource. That's a point constantly made by the MLM (multilevel marketing) people -- which are scams in my opinion. But the comfort Chinese people have mixing friendship and business is one big reason that MLM is hugely popular in China. Unfortunately, MLM tends to ruin people's finances, and therefore seriously strain friendships. But the idea that MLM pushes of "don't let your network of friendship just sit idle" is a very valid one, at least if you can make yourself comfortable with the idea.

Chinese people are also quite meticulous about keeping accounts of which of their friends is worthy of their friendship. Americans can joke about some people being "frienemies" or "moochers"; in the Chinese world, such people would be very quickly thrown out of any social circles where they practiced that kind of behavior. That is also true of Chinese extended families. While extended families serve as mutual-assistance and credit societies, being biologically related to the family is only a necessary, but not sufficient, condition for membership in the network of mutual assistance. You also have to be pulling your own weight, or had to have pulled your own weight in the past. Perhaps the closest thing to this would be the Italian American mafia, especially as portrayed in movies like *Godfather*; everyone is related, either literally by blood or metaphorically by "blood oaths," but you have to keep contributing or else you'll be pushed out (or off a bridge!), even if you are closely related by blood.

Americans sometimes call that "pruning," or "contacts pruning." Get rid of people who are a drain on you and contribute nothing. It sounds cold-hearted to Americans, but it's very much the Chinese way of life. That's also why Chinese people will not -- absent some strong other reason -- befriend someone who is poor, or disabled, or otherwise unfortunate, because that person is seen as not being able to pull their weight in the friendship. And a Chinese friendship, like a Chinese marriage or family relation, is about practical assistance, not about sharing happy moments together.

Like a boss: Chinese employment

Say you're a fry cook somewhere in the United States. Life isn't that great. You're making around minimum wage. But life is pretty simple, in that you know that at the end of every pay period, you'll get paid for your wage times the number of hours worked (minus taxes). If the business is having trouble, your future hourly salary might be reduced (as long as it's still at least minimum wage), and your hours might be cut (hooray, more free time). But other than that, you're pretty well insulated from the ups and downs of your boss's business. As the saying goes about the plumber's mantra: "All you need to know is shit flows downhill and Friday is payday."

In China, a low-level worker such as a fry cook, especially in a small business, is really "like a boss" -- but in the worst sense. If the business doesn't do well, he doesn't get paid. If a customer complains, the refund will come out of his salary. If customers stay longer than the official opening hours, the employee has to stay too, without any hope for compensation. Uniforms and supplies are of course the employee's own responsibility to buy . And so on.

What's the flip side of that, from the Chinese boss's perspective? A Chinese boss assumes that every one of his employees wants to be a business owner, and is only saving up money, experience, and contacts (guanxi) to open his own business, very likely in the same market segment as his current boss's business. Perhaps for historical reasons and the culture of small-scale entrepreneurism, every Chinese person, traditionally, wants to be an entrepreneur and boss, and finds the concept of salaried employment quite foreign. Additionally, along the lines of low levels of trust, the boss thinks, "why should my employee put in any effort if I pay him his salary no matter how well business goes?"

There is no real labor law enforcement in China, and noncompete agreements exist for foreigners and for very high-level positions, but for any other employee, it is more or less assumed that everyone is just biding time while trying to figure out how to start a competing business. I go to one small Chinese-owned restaurant in New York, offering quite a specialized and not-really-Chinese menu, where the Chinese owner, in contravention of federal and state law, refuses to hire any Chinese staff. Her thinking? Every Chinese person she's ever hired has started a competing business after a few months of working at the original business and learning how to do things. Non-Chinese people, according to this owner anyway, lack that kind of entrepreneurial desire.

This same restaurant owner hires a non-Chinese woman as her family's housekeeper and nanny in her home, despite some of the people living in the home (the boss's parents) only speaking Chinese. I asked her if she was able to find a Chinese(-speaking) housekepeer. She explained to me: "If a Chinese person is washing the floor, they will always be thinking about how they are too good to be washing floors, and will resent you for hiring them to do that job, and will be planning how to use the floor-washing job as a stepping stone to start a business so they don't have to wash floors anymore." Her words, not mine, and of course a heavy dose of stereotyping, but also some cultural truth.

In China, it's well known that the ripoff Starbucks copy shops were started by people who worked at Starbucks for a few months to learn the business -- and similarly with fake McDonalds, fake Gucci, and many similar examples. It is more or less assumed that if an employee at a successful shop of that sort doesn't have some strong reason to the contrary (say, they are currently in school, studying to become a physician), they are planning how to start their own version of your business.

If you're going to be hiring Chinese people, in China or outside it, be aware of the "like a boss" mentality and your employees' expectations. I don't suggest that in the U.S. you withhold your employees' pay if the business isn't doing well, but Chinese employees are very well attuned to profit sharing, even if in traditional Chinese culture it's more opaque and less defined than formal profit-sharing agreements sometimes used in the US. Even a janitor or fry cook will very much appreciate being made "like a boss" and having a share -- even if a risky share, with the Chinese love of gambling -- in the business.

This goes somewhat against the well-known idea that Chinese culture is built on hierarchy. Of course it is, and of course unequal power and hierarchy is a big part of the reason that employees can't expect anything like minimum wage and labor protections. But for every action, there's a reaction, and the flip side of the hierarchy is the insubservience that I call "like a boss" -- the idea that because the boss's position is so privileged, everyone is trying hard to become a boss. Maybe if China were like Scandinavia or even the United States, where employees are relatively equal with the boss, there would be less of a desire for everyone to become a boss.

This "like a boss" attitude extends not only to individual employees, but also to contractors. Just as individual employees are known for taking the boss's concept and connections and starting a competing business, contractors are known for -- and in fact would be considered foolish for not taking advantage of -- using their clients' connections and know-how to make knock-off or at least competing products. This is also why Chinese firms prefer to do manufacturing in-house rather than contracting out to an independent factory: at least if the manufacturing is in-house, you only have to contend with your factory manager who might want to take the design and employees and tooling and start a competing factory, rather than deal with an already established factory business that might want to do the same.

Trademark, copyright, noncompetition laws, and unjust enrichment laws? In China, they exist only on paper, if at all. Enforcement does sometimes happen, when the Chinese authorities get a phone call from a foreign company whom they want to impress, and do some symbolic "crackdowns" -- but in real, everyday business life, any risk of legal prosecution is the farthest thing from anyone's mind.

Taxes, laws, and other trivial matters

"In China, if you don't pay taxes, you're a smart guy. In America, if you don't pay taxes, you're a bad guy." I was having lunch with my father's friend from Shanghai, who has now become a successful grocery wholesaler in New York. I asked him what the biggest difference is between grocery wholesaling in China and America. That was his first answer. And while I'm not sure whether it's really the biggest difference, it is one big difference. A big part of the Chinese method of doing business is figuring out how to stay clear of any laws and regulations that aren't beneficial. Remember that our mind is always on our money and our money is on our minds? Any arguments about fairness just don't stand up to a Chinese person's basic desire to hold on to "their" money.

Worker safety regulations? Minimum wage? Immigration restrictions? Freely ignored, unless there's an immediate threat of enforcement on the horizon. Part of the reason is that traditionally, China didn't have any such regulations. Bosses beat their workers and workers' recourse was very limited. Chinese communism came along and instituted worker protection regulations on paper -- but the reality was that "enforcement" of these regulations consisted of regularly collecting protection money from businesses, and the "enforcers" of these laws believed in the laws themselves just as little as the business people did.

Mainland Chinese people have never had a government or system of laws that is "by the people, of the people, for the people," despite communist rhetoric to the contrary. No one in the "People's Republic of" China would ever believe that the laws and regulations exist for common good. Everybody knows the system is rigged, and when the system holds no moral legitimacy with the people, evading the system isn't seen as morally wrong. It's seen as potentially risky, but not immoral. Everybody knows that the tax authorities are just trying to get rich by cheating you, and everybody knows that you're going to do your best to cheat them back (although they hold all the power, and the degree to which you can "cheat them back" is minuscule).

If you want to know what Chinese people think of their government's regulations, you may want to listen to the song "Everybody Knows," by Leonard Cohen. A professor played this song for us in an MBA class about crony capitalism, and it has stuck with me, although it's awfully depressing:

Everybody knows that the dice are loaded
Everybody rolls with their fingers crossed
Everybody knows that the war is over
Everybody knows the good guys lost
Everybody knows the fight was fixed
The poor stay poor, the rich get rich
That's how it goes
Everybody knows

This is the attitude of everyone from a poor farmer to a middle-class accountant to the richest tycoon or party boss. Of course, the tycoon or party boss believes that he has to some extent effectively played the system -- but there is no tycoon or party boss in China who doesn't carry some grievance of how the corrupt system is rigged against him. And in large part it goes back to how money is everything. A government official may even start out with some faith in the law as written (although this is rare) -- but when buying a house, sending his children to school, and keeping his wife requires him to have the $5,000/month unofficial income that all his colleagues have, rather than the $500/month income his salary offers, what is he do? Not to mention that in most Chinese government jobs, higher-ups are always pressuring their front-line staff for kickbacks on *their* collected kickbacks. An honest, non-bribe-taking government official isn't going to get very far in China's government.

What about China before communism? The situation was much the same, although back then, it was not considered corruption -- perhaps because there was not yet a show of playing by Western standards of "clean government." In pre-communist China, government officials usually received no salary, only sometimes a small living allowance (rice and a mat to sleep on) -- and were expected to collect "tributes" from the citizens they served. This wasn't seen as corruption, as I said. It was only expressing gratitude or an exchange of favors.

So when it's universally understood that laws and regulations are just another game played for money, there's no honor to losing. The only thing to do is win. And winning means not following any of those laws and regulations imposed by greedy officials.

The situation is more complex than simply "Chinese people don't follow the law." Chinese people will follow the law when they have a sense of being closely tracked and watched -- as most people, most businesses, and most situations are closely tracked by the government (in some form) in China. Any sort of self-reporting, self-policing, or "honor system" simply doesn't exist in China. No one in China would honestly pay taxes or follow any other regulation simply because "it's the right thing to do," without fear of a harsh penalty for noncompliance.

Do Chinese people living in the United States follow the same ethic? To a large part, yes, it's true for people who spent their lives in China before coming to the US. People's thinking doesn't instantly change the moment they move to another country or take a citizenship oath. That's not true of everybody, but is true to some extent. Is it true of ethnically Chinese people in the US? It's probably true for them to the same degree that they've retained other aspects of China in the way they do business.

A friend of mine is a lawyer. A client of his had his parked car hit and seriously damaged by one of the New York "Chinese bus" services, the buses that very cheaply take people between New York and other East Coast US cities. Of course, the Chinese bus didn't have insurance -- or actually, it did have insurance, but the insurance the bus had was for a personal vehicle, not for a commercial bus taking passengers for hire, so the insurance coverage was not valid. (Here we go again: Chinese business people saving money no matter what the regulations say.) My lawyer friend's first instinct was to sue the driver of the bus, the company that was leasing the bus to the Chinese tour company, and the parking garage where the collision happened. I asked him why he doesn't consider suing the Chinese-owned-and-operated company that actually operated the bus, which is the party that would normally be the first target for a lawsuit? He laughed as if I'd just proposed something ludicrous. "Any lawyer will tell you, Chinese companies never pay judgments," he told me. A Chinese company -- and that means a company primarily operated by people from China, no matter where the actual company -- would simply ignore the lawsuit and the ensuing court judgment, and if any efforts were put forth to collect on the judgment (for example, seizing the company's bank accounts), the company would close down and then likely re-open with a new name and new official ownership. A lawsuit judgment, like any form of government authority, is to be avoided, if you want to hold on to your money Chinese-style. Certainly, in China, the judgment-avoiding process would start even earlier than that, with perhaps a fake license plate on the bus, or an immediate bribe to police and court to "forget" the identity of the bus or to dismiss the case on a technicality or some such.

Anything related to the law is not only seen as interference from greedy officials, but is seen as a matter of courting favor with the correct people and obtaining the correct paperwork -- which is the case in China, both contemporary and pre-communist. I recall an acquaintance originally from Hong Kong, now living in New York, who asked me for help with a complicated real estate investment matter, involving payment, ownership, loans, and property taxes on several condos in New York. This acquaintance is a Cantonese speaker, and I don't speak Cantonese, so we communicate in English.

I kept asking her about each condo: "Who owns this one?" and she would give me an answer in the form of "it's under my daughter's trust company's name." And I kept asking -- "ok, I understand what the papers say, but who really owns this?" And she would go into a detailed story of "in whose name" this was and "the name on the documents" for taxes, mortgage, this and that. Apparently her daughter, a US citizen (by course of "birth tourism," another topic altogether) was receiving some kind of preferred loan as a first-time homebuyer. But when I asked whether the daughter was actually involved in the deal, she looked at me as if I'm crazy -- of course not! The daughter doesn't know or doesn't care. It's only "in her name." And who was actually living there? Some other Chinese person, "under the name" of yet another Chinese person. For Western culture, that's identity theft. For Chinese culture, that's the normal culture of dealing with bureaucracy.

In China, the important thing in dealing with the government is obtaining a proper chop. I recall the same woman, when she was asking me about why the IRS was sending her inquiry letters when she had paid her taxes, assuring me that her taxes are all paid up, and showing me her (Chinese) accountant's documentation of the amount due in taxes, and a payment in that amount having been submitted to the IRS. I told her that the amount due that's shown is meaningless if it's predicated on an untrue report of income. She insisted that she has this piece of paper that shows that her taxes are all paid, and she was going to show this letter to the IRS if they allege that her taxes are not paid. When I asked her whether she truthfully reported all her income to the IRS, of course she looked at me as if I were crazy. Who would ever do such a thing? The important thing is getting the piece of paper.

Hence the well-known Hong Kong (and also mainland Chinese) proclivity for extremely complicated legal structures and shell companies and other such things. In American law, there is a doctrine of "substance over form" or another doctrine of "economic reality," meaning that the substance and economic reality of what is actually happening -- for example, who is actually living in and paying for a condo -- is what is important, and not what some document says or whose "name" is being used for something.

Another friend of mine was producing a high-end electronic device. Kickstarter type stuff. He got an order for several units of it from a company in China. Of course, he knew that the Chinese company was likely to copy the design (that's another matter altogether), but he didn't care, because they were going to pay him enough for those units, and anyway, he knew that no matter, someone would eventually copy the design.

Anyway, the Chinese prospective customer, apparently never having ordered anything from the United States, said that before they tendered payment, they needed to see that this device was "certified" by the US government. Such a "certification" from the US government would not only make them feel better, but would be a useful marketing tool for them. My friend at first thought to explain to them that in general, the US government doesn't "certify" products (unless that product specifically requires some sort of certification). But he knew that the Chinese party likely wouldn't believe him and would back out of the deal. So what did he do? He approached his county's economic development and job creation board, and asked them to write him an official letter congratulating him on his excellent product. They obliged, and sent him a congratulatory letter on official letterhead. My friend scanned and emailed the letter to the Chinese client -- and they were tremendously happy and impressed that indeed this product had the "correct chop" and was "certified."

Indeed, in China, obtaining such a "chop" would consist of knowing somebody and paying a bribe, but Chinese people assume (half-correctly) that the US government issues such "chops" to the best products, based on objective standards, and without corruption. Of course, they're half-correct, because while you're unlikely to be successful attempting a federal government official, the US business and regulatory culture doesn't have a litany of government seals, stamps, chops, permits, and licenses necessary to do anything. If you hear an American complaining about necessary paperwork to do business in the US -- they have never seen China!

Having the right "chop" extends not to just to government, but to all aspects of business. In another book of mine, I told the story of a Canadian teacher of mine in China who was trying to explain the concept of brands and branding to his Chinese students, as if we had never heard of the concept -- when not only are Chinese people infamously brand-obsessed, but ancient China most likely invented the concept of brands. Just as with government paperwork, having the right brand on a product, a system, a degree, an employee, or an organization is crucial for any Chinese business or consumer.

What's really real: brand, image, and judging a book by its cover

Ancient China invented "chops," stamps that carried the unique brand of the official or the businessperson who would vouch for the authenticity of a document or a product. As I recollected in my book about Asian fetishes, about ten years ago, hordes of "smart" Westerners showed up in China, believing that they were going to teach us naive Chinese people about the idea of branding -- when in fact branding was (most likely, if you believe the historians) invented in ancient China. In fact, China is and was completely obsessed with brands. Even during the deepest throes of hardline Maoism (which is now making a comeback, but that's another story), people were obsessed with showing off their political, ideological, and guanxi brands. Nowadays that's been supplemented by showing off product brands.

Take a walk around the campus of Harvard University, and you can be assured of one constant sight: groups of tourists from mainland China posing with, and especially having their children pose with, the statue of John Harvard and various signs that say Harvard University. People misinterpret this as a sign of China's love for education. I don't think so at all. I don't think there's any love of education. I think it's all about the brand.

Nowadays, there's a similar trend at Oxford and Cambridge universities, especially as China's government has been trying to encourage more Chinese students to study in the UK as opposed to the US (although the Communist Party bigshots still universally send their kids to US schools). A

Chinese soap opera featured Cambridge University, and hordes of tourists take their photos there, often playing at being British students.

Do you still not believe me when I say this is entirely a story about branding, and not about education? Milan Kundera famously liked to ask men whether they would prefer to be seen on the town with a supermodel but not be able to have sex with her, or to have sex with her but never be seen anywhere with her. According to Kundera, men will claim that they prefer the latter, but if they are actually presented with the choice in real life, they will always choose the former. Well, if you ask Chinese people -- would you prefer to have a Harvard education but no diploma (nor any other mention or proof of your education), or would you prefer to have a Harvard diploma without ever having attended any Harvard classes -- I am confident that almost every Chinese person and family will choose the diploma without the education.

"What would you study at Harvard?" you can ask. The universal answer will be: "How to get rich." Or: "It doesn't matter." It is no surprise -- and I gather this from friends who are graduate students and professors at Harvard and similar schools -- that a great majority of students from mainland China are entirely interested in the brand power of the diploma, and don't care about the studied material any further than as some hoops to jump through in order to get the diploma. That's fine, and there are students of all nationalities that have that attitude. But "a great Chinese love of education" this is not. Unless by education you mean the power of having the Harvard brand associated with your name -- which is also perhaps what Chinese people mean when they say they love education.

People have brands. And what famous brands you can be associated with has a lot to do with your status in Chinese society. In Japanese society, at the peak of the salaryman culture and economic stability, an honorific way to address someone would be by the company they worked for, at least if that company was seen as big and prestigious. In that Japanese culture, your friends might be known as Toyota-san, Shinsei-san, and Toshiba-san. Their jobs *are* their identities and their brands. While China doesn't have anything that explicit, there is a very strong idea that whatever big, strong institutions you're associated with determine your social and economic worth. They're your brand. And your prestigious brands might include the city of your birth, the political or business status of your parents, the university you attended (of course), the big company you work for, and the branded products that you own.

In fact, if there's anything in China similar to the Toyota/Shinsei/Toshiba-san culture of Japan, it's not totally unusual to refer to people by their favorite brands or possessions: a guy who drives a Mercedes easily gets the nickname "Benz" and a woman who carries many Louis Vuitton bags might be called "Elvie." Sounds crass, right? But to the Chinese mind, these famous company brands are affirmations of these people's worth. Remember: there's no separation between the commercial and the personal. Not only should you do business with your friends, but your friends should befriend you because of your employment and what you own. "I won't be that guy's friend; he drives an economy car and went to community college" would be a statement met with strong reprimand in most American social circles, but in China, it would be completely normal -- after all, a friend who doesn't have much money or brand is not worth much, and most likely can't help you much.

As is the case anywhere in the world, some people have it all, and others don't. There are lots of Chinese people who were born in Shanghai, studied at Oxford, drive a Bentley, and wear a Patek Philippe, or whatever combination you want to put together. But there are lots of people who can't do all that. And so there is the very common Chinese phenomenon of having a "trophy item." Your trophy item is the *one* very prestigious thing you can associate yourself with, and you hope that your social worth is determined just by your being associated with this item, and not by all the other lacking areas in your life.

This explains why high-end smartphones, particularly the newest iphones, are tremendously popular in China, and why few Chinese people want any phone other than an iphone. It's not primarily a communications device for them. It's not even a computing or photo-taking device. It's purely a status device. $1,000 for a high-end iphone 6 sounds like a lot of money, because it is. But $1,000 if a cheap way to get a really great trophy item. After all, the iphone 6 is the newest and the best. And compared with the cost of a Harvard degree, or a new BMW, or a fancy condo, or a model wife, $1,000 is very, very affordable.

You may have heard stories, either from China or from Chinese communities in the U.S., about someone who lives in a dirt-floored metal shack and his only possession is an iphone 6 that is worth more than his shack. Or someone who lives in an urban tenement and can't afford to buy shoes but leases a high-end luxury car. Or -- quite commonly in China these days -- a young woman from a poor background who turns to prostitution to pay for her expensive handbags. All these are examples not of greed or of luxury consumption or of messed-up priorities, but of "trophy items" intended to buy social status. And you can get more social status by getting just one trophy item and pretty much neglecting spending on anything else, rather than doing some middling spending on several things. (As with several aspects of Chinese culture, there is a remarkable similarity here to American ghetto culture: in stereotypes, and sometimes in reality, American ghetto residents are said to live in slum apartments and spend their money on jewelry and luxury cars to show off. And maybe the social reasons are quite similar.)

If you're selling branded items, the rise of budgets in China is a big deal and a great opportunity. A product's just being foreign is already a big brand in itself. A Chinese acquaintance of mine runs a phone and electronics store in Chinatown. Once when I was getting my phone repaired at his shop, he told me with frustration that when Chinese immigrants want to buy an electronic device or laptop at his shop and he asks them which one they want, all they want is one "made in the USA." They are in disbelief when he tells them that there are no laptops or phones made in the USA nowadays. He then offers them something he knows will work -- he asks them whether they want a laptop from Dell, an American company, with a prominent Dell logo on the cover. Yes, a million times yes!

And if you're going to be in a position where Chinese people are trying to impress you, especially in a business setting, you have to be aware of the brands they're trying to associate themselves with, and appropriately acknowledge and compliment how excellent those brands are. If your new boss buys a new Samsung phone, in America it would be acceptable to point out that this phone lacks some key feature or is overpriced -- but in China, it is crucial to compliment the phone and of course comment on its high price, because the phone is an extension of its owner.

If you plan on selling yourself (not *that* way, perv) in China or to Chinese people, you'd better be very aware of what your brand is. Chinese people will absolutely think less of you because your clothes, watch, and phone aren't made by famous, high-class manufacturers. A Chinese friend of mine went to graduate school in the US, receiving a PhD, and then working as an assistant professor at a US university. She then went back to China to be a visiting professor. What her colleagues and her students most noticed about her: not her research, not her credentials, not her fluency with high-level mathematics, but... that she wore a $30 Casio watch. In fact, her supervisor in China specifically told her that if she wants to be respected, she has to wear a more prestigious watch. Never mind that she is a lab researcher and high-end watches and lab chemicals shouldn't mix, and never mind that she had a top PhD from a top program. (Unfortunately, her PhD is from an academically excellent university that is unheard of in China, so she only gains credibility from having a degree "from America.")

If you have your branding in order, then you're pretty much all set for selling yourself (hey, stop giggling) in China. That is indeed how many foreigners catapulted themselves into positions and situations in China that they would've never qualified for back in their home countries. Graduated from Harvard (even if an unrelated field and without any distinction)? Mopped floors at Goldman Sachs for a year? Have a

Rolex? Welcome to China -- you're our new CEO! This is actually not that much of an exaggeration. On the other hand, if you attended, say, Caltech (an excellent school which holds almost no name recognition in China), successfully founded and managed a small and non-famous investment firm, and wear a Timex watch -- welcome to China, and maybe you can be an English teacher. Maybe.

In fact, being racially white, Caucasian, of European descent, used to be enough of a powerful brand in China on its own. As I'll mention in the chapter on views of foreigners, that view is slowly changing as foreigners become else rare in China, but whiteness still does carry some branding power. This is why many Chinese consumer products have English-language names, instructions written in nonsense English, and photos on the label of white people smiling.

It's all summed up pretty well by the idea of judging a book by its cover. Putting your best face forward is in Western culture considered showing off, but in Chinese (and much of East Asian) culture, it's merely showing your status to others, much like wearing an identifying badge of who you are. Everyone is always assumed to be putting on their best face -- or an embellished version of it -- and showing the best aspects of their brand. That's not showing off; it's only the natural Chinese way of being. And a person who can afford a Rolex but wears a Casio, or who, like my ex-boyfriend in New York, can afford a mansion but lives in a rent-controlled apartment, is not thrifty but weird or crazy or devious.

When I was an MBA student, during a school break when I returned to China, a group of Chinese entrepreneurs (in real estate, of course) in Shanghai offered me $1,000 USD to do a few investment presentations for them. They told me that they had a lead on some not-too-expensive land outside of Shanghai, and they are trying to raise money to buy that land and build a condo building on it. Sounded fine. They wanted me to do the pitch because I carried prestige and credibility because of the brand of my being an MBA student at a famous US university.

And then they showed me the materials that they wanted me to present. There were clearly Photoshopped images of the apartment building on this piece of land. According to the materials they wanted me to present to potential investors, they had acquired the land two years ago and already built the building, and now just need investment for the final touches of the business. I wanted to give them the ethical benefit of the doubt and asked them if these materials were for use later, after the land has been acquired and the building built. No, of course not, they told me: the materials were for use now.

I asked the painfully obvious question: you guys don't even have the land, and you want to tell your investors that you already bought the land and even constructed a building on it? The reaction I got from them was as if I had pointed out a minor typo somewhere in the appendices. "Oh, don't worry about that detail. We'll get the land." I, having never done business in China, and having been schooled over and over in my MBA program about how easy it is to get handcuffs and an orange jumpsuit, asked them, "So why don't you just *tell* your investors that the land is a sure thing but hasn't been bought yet?" And of course their answer was a combination of "we need to tell them what they want to hear" and "we can't kill the deal by making ourselves look inexperienced" and "what's the difference, if we're going to buy the land anyway." Just for curiosity's sake, I asked them what they plan to do when the investors inevitably go in person to see the building? "We'll tell them they went to the wrong address," one of the partners went. "No, we'll explain to them that we haven't built it yet," said another partner. They hadn't gone this far in planning their conspiracy to defraud -- by first-world standards, anyway -- some investors of something like twenty million dollars. I refused the $1,000 they were offering me and refused to do this kind of pitch, which they took as a sign that I'd been corrupted by America. Maybe indeed I had been. I would not be surprised if they got some stand-in for me and claimed that the stand-in was a US MBA student.

In China, this isn't a funny story about some bumbling scammers. Other than the bumbling part and them not having quite figured out how to answer investors' questions, it's how business is normally done. And no one sees an ethical problem with it, except perhaps foreigners who aren't expecting it. The basic unwritten but ironclad rule is: show your best face, even if it's not quite your face. In the world of investments, official proclamations from companies are known to be only loosely based on the truth, and rarely if ever include any gloomy predictions or notes about problems in the business -- and this is not because publicly traded Chinese companies lack difficulties! Openly talking yourself down is simply not done in the business world, in contradiction to the frequent Western belief (and model-minority myth) that Chinese people are "modest" or "honest."

Many US-based small business people are entranced by the idea of importing some knicknack from China and selling it at huge profits in the US, or whatever other first-world market. They go online and find Alibaba or Taobao or some manufacturer's site, with lots of beautiful photos of whatever the product is going to be. And they believe there's no risk, because they order a sample from the factory, placing a small order before placing the big order. Well, as any Chinese factory employee will tell you, as basic primary lseson of business, is that the samples are made completely separately from the regular production runs. Sometimes the samples are bought from some other factory, or sometimes are made with extraordinary care, or sometimes are made when the tooling is new, or sometimes are simply the "best of the batch" hand-selected from production runs. In any case, all the samples demonstrate is what kind of product the factory believes foreign buyers will like.

What else other than samples? Every factory will have a long list of certifications and awards it received. ISO this and that, International this and that, and so on. All fake. Varying degrees and methods of fakeness -- whether bought from another factory, or bought with a bribe, or created with photoshop, or whatever else works -- but all universally fake. They are as fake as the fancy university degrees the management and their children claim to have. It doesn't matter.

I've told you a valuable tip about Chinese factories. You're welcome. But there's a very similar thing going on with Chinese people in dating relationships. Both men and women think it's best to show their best side -- often embellished -- to attract a spouse. Most single men carry a folder on their phone that has photos of (allegedly) their car, their condo, their office, their university degree, and their bank statement. This is used for showing to prospective brides they might meet somewhere. A single man's parents carry similar photos to show to parents of prospective brides. And women? Their bodies are already their "best faces forward," especially when Chinese men believe they can visually identify virgins. (There are actually "virginity certificates" available from doctors, to present to prospective husbands -- but I must admit they are not a common thing to see, as hilarious as it would be if I could tell you that they're universally used.)

Chinese women have a saying about men: When a man is courting you to marry him, he is a mouse; after you marry him, he is a general. And Chinese men have similar sayings about women turning into "house dragons" after marriage.

No Chinese allowed: foreigners are easier

Americans are accustomed to the sight of Chinatowns, such as those in New York or San Francisco, and often make the assumption upon seeing those Chinatowns that Chinese people only like to associate with other Chinese people. That's an oversimplification, and to some extent, it's exactly the opposite of reality.

This isn't a book on the history of American Chinatowns, but two things are important to remember about why Chinese people ended up living in clustered communities. First, there was a large degree of exclusion, not inclusion. (In fact, there was a law called the Chinese Exclusion Act, which excluded Chinese immigrants from the entire United States.) The Chinatowns were usually the tenements and undesirable neighborhoods that were the only places that would accept Chinese residents. Language also excluded new immigrants. Whether or not they wanted to associate with other Chinese immigrants, the other Chinese immigrants were the only people with whom they could speak a common language (sometimes). The second aspect of this, which is more important, is that Chinese people didn't just settle down with any of their Chinese countrymen. All the American Chinatowns, in their various incarnations over the years, consisted of tightly knit communities from China choosing to stick together. Most American Chinatowns originally consisted of people from just one county -- Taishan County in Guangdong Province -- and often from just one or two villages in that county. And within the Chinatown, each tenement building or block or street was generally dominated by an extended family, again, sticking together.

It wasn't a matter of "We're all Chinese, so let's stick together." It was more a matter of "We were lifelong friends and neighbors in China, so let's continue being friends and neighbors in America." In the varying levels of guanxi relationship, there is one specific level for people from the same place as you -- usually defined as the same village -- and the term sounds like "laoxiang." Keep in mind that with China's long history, where you're from is most likely where your family has lived for hundreds if not thousands of years, and in almost any village, there is a widely acknowledged degree of consanguinity (shared bloodlines). When we Chinese city dwellers sometimes joke about a "bumpkin" or "redneck" village in China, one thing we say about it is that everyone in the village has the same surname -- which is more or less true in the typical Chinese village.

So being from a certain village is more meaningful in the Chinese sensibility than the American sensibility of, say, "I'm from Connecticut," which means that you grew up in Connecticut, and maybe your parents moved to Connecticut at some point in their lives, from another state or another country, and unless you're a Native American, your grandparents or great-grandparents definitely were not from Connecticut and not even from America.

I'm telling you all this to prove my point that when you see Chinese people clustered together, it doesn't mean that they particularly like to deal with other Chinese people. The general opinion, among Chinese people, of doing business with Chinese people is that they are good because they will do you favors once guanxi is established, but that you stand a very high risk of being cheated, and that Chinese people, as compared to non-

Chinese people, are tough (demanding, complaining) customers. Talk to any recent immigrant shopkeeper in a Chinatown -- as I've done sometimes -- and foremost on his or her list of ambitions is getting out of Chinatown in order to stop dealing with all these Chinese people.

As a rule of thumb, Chinese people most like dealing with their close friends and relatives, of course. But barring that, they would rather deal with "American" (meaning: white) strangers than with Chinese strangers -- because the standard of behavior shown by "Americans" toward strangers is much higher than that shown by Chinese people toward strangers. While it's best to deal with people in your circle of guanxi, absent guanxi, it's known (or believed) that foreigners will have some sense of moral obligation not to take advantage of strangers, while Chinese people will have absolutely no such sense of obligation absent a personal relationship or a direct risk of punishment.

Stupid but instructive example: Take a look on Ebay. Find any seller in China. Almost always, they explicitly prohibit orders from customers in China and Chinese-dominated countries. The original intent of the feature on Ebay is to avoid countries where it's too expensive to ship. For a vendor in China, it's unlikely that shipping within China is more costly than shipping abroad. But the real obstacle is in fact not shipping but a mistrust of other Chinese people.

A Chinese immigrant acquaintance of mine in New York is an insurance agent. I asked him why he doesn't advertise his business in the Chinese newspapers. He told me he avoids Chinese customers as much as possible, because they always try to cheat him, and see insurance as a game of trying to get the

60

most "payoff" from the insurance company (otherwise known as insurance fraud in American culture).

Beyond that, for the past decades, white-skinned foreigners have been seen by Chinese people as not only being trustworthy (or really, childlike and naive, so as not to take advantage of other people) but also very rich. I remember my parents telling me a story of watching American TV some twenty years ago and being shocked that there were people in America -- white people no less -- who couldn't afford to eat. That belief still exists, although it's not as prevalent as it was some ten or twenty years ago. Now it's more common to believe that foreigners aren't really rich, but are more willing to part with their money. Everyone in the US knows that China holds a great deal of US government debt; that fact is constantly trumpeted by China's government and media as proof that Westerners make a lot of money but don't know how to save or manage it.

As a footnote to the above, there has been a recent upsurge in the Chinese belief that Jews -- yes, the Hebrew people -- are some kind of special secret society with magical powers over money. In the Western world, "theories" like that are considered ridiculous and fringe conspiracy-theory stuff, but in China, they are very commonly believed, perhaps because very few Chinese people have (knowingly) had any contact with Jews. According to these theories, American Jews -- who by the way are not considered real Americans in the Chinese mindset -- are particularly dangerous and powerful because they combine the American ability to earn money but also have the Chinese characteristic of "our minds on our money, our money on our minds." If you go to a Chinese bookstore and look for books about personal finance, you will see many titles about, well, Jews. Or purportedly about Jews. And there is one particular book called *Currency Wars* -- written by a man with absolutely no education or experience in finance or economics -- that claims that Jews manipulate global currency markets.

Upshot of this obsession with Jewishness for you practically for dealing with Chinese people? If you happen to be Jewish, or even if not, be very aware of how strong the associations and prejudices will be if you mention your Jewish heritage or religion. It's not something to take lightly, and it's way beyond what you might expect in America, some harmless jokes about penny-pinching and bagels. First, if you are Jewish, Chinese people will consider you "not really American," and second, they will consider you sort of a dark wizard of the financial arts -- tremendously skilled, but perhaps too wily to be trusted. If you are trying to get a job in finance in China, or gain any kind of credibility about your business skill to Chinese people, Jewishness can be a powerful brand. But if you declare yourself as Jewish, you might lose all the positive impressions you might otherwise have had, of you being an "American."

That's a piece of a larger cultural belief in China, that "Americans," who are very much a brand in themselves, are only white people of Anglo-Saxon heritage, with Anglo-Saxon names. That most likely has to do with China having had a 4,000 year history, and Chinese people being able to trace back their histories and families and identities thousands of years within China -- while an American might fully consider himself an American, and be called an American by other Americans, but have lived in America for perhaps only a few years, and often not have white skin or an Anglo name. This may be another bit of information with which you may want to be careful. If, say, your grandparents came to New York from Russia and you mention this to your Chinese colleagues or customers, you will forever become known as "the Russian," not "the American." Never mind of course that any American other than a Native American has a similar family history. (In fact, I've often wondered whether average Chinese people would consider Native Americans to be Americans -- perhaps they'd be considered "touren," which is a Chinese word that means something like "local savages.")

If you don't have white skin or an Anglo name, you can not partake of the American brand prestige in China or with Chinese people. Even if your grandparents came from Hoiping, China in the 1800s to build railroads and your family has been in the United States for over one hundred years, you will always be considered "Chinese" by Chinese people. No matter what you say, and no matter what your passport says. The term "American" in your US passport is to this Chinese mindset only a matter of citizenship, a chop that you can obtain and fix, and not a substantive difference of who you are. Remember my mention of Chinese people's use of "names" and fictitious and complicated business forms? They consider nonwhite people who are US citizens to be engaging in something along these lines.

The practical advice is that if you are not white and you plan on doing business in China, you will face an uphill journey, you will not easily be able to brand yourself as an American, and you have to brand yourself somehow. It's fairly common for Chinese Americans and other non-white-skinned people to hire some very blonde, blue-eyed, Anglo-named person to be the "face" of their business or other venture in China, even if that person has no actual knowledge or credibility in the field, other than their umm, racial purity.

I need to specifically tell you these things about how Chinese people see you and your racial brand because Westerners generally are less concerned with and less aware of how others see and evaluate them. It's a frequent statement by teenagers and even non-teenagers that you don't care what anyone thinks, that you want to express and not impress, and so on. There's also the Western belief in seeing the prince behind the frog, and the moral and intellectual value of seeing something that's not obvious at the surface. There's no such belief in China, at least when judging people's worth. If someone rejects you for a job or even for a friendship because you have dark skin and are use a Nokia phone, they are just being smart, not being shallow, at least in the Chinese social context and to Chinese standards. Don't expect Chinese people to see beyond the cover and your skin color and racial heritage (or perceived racial heritage) in evaluating you. Don't feel shy about showing off your credentials or your wealth or whatever else -- because in the Chinese world, you have to wear this stuff on your sleeve.

On the other hand, if you are a white American, welcome to the land of white privilege as never imagined by even your wildest Tumblr social justice warrior fantasies. You will to a large extent be assumed to be quite rich and accomplished. And you will be assumed to be excellent at book learning and technology, but not so good at street smarts -- sounds quite like white stereotypes of Asian Americans, doesn't it? You will be assumed to treat strangers well, and to be generous in a childlike way. In fact, white people are quite generally believed to be childlike: maybe good at formal knowledge, but lacking knowledge of the ways of the world. And white people's perceived honesty is not a result of them being better people, but seen as a form of their being childlike and not yet caught up on the ways of the world.

Also it will be believed that in regard to money you: spend and borrow money, never give any money to your elderly parents nor to your adult children, did not pay for your children's education, split all bills 50/50 even between spouses, spend a great deal of money on wine, count on government social security for retirement, and strongly prefer products made in Western countries over products made in Asia. I remember my friends and relatives asking what kind of car my white American boyfriend drives in the US, and when I told them he drives a Toyota, they asked why he can't afford an American or European made car? There's a deep-seated belief that products "made by white people" (the assumption, of course, that everyone working in a factory in the US or Germany is white) are far superior to "products made by Asians." I already mentioned the story of how Chinese people demand to buy a "made in USA" ipad or iphone, and are outraged that no such product is available.

Some Americans who are familiar with the history of racial discrimination against ethnic minority populations in the United States assume that countries where white, European-descent people are a minority must have a similar degree of discrimination against white people. Yet it just doesn't happen that way. White people are seen as a little bit childlike and soft and spoiled, but if there's a stereotype about them and their abilities, generally those stereotypes have to do with them being in all manner superior. And definitely, in business dealings, white people are seen as much more trustworthy than fellow Chinese people.

In fact, it is well known that con artists and scammers in China hire white people -- often backpackers desperate for money -- to be the "face" of the business, and do the "pitch," much as I (because of my American MBA credentials) was hired to do the "pitch" for the dodgy real estate investment deal I earlier mentioned. Everybody knows that a scam pitched by a white person never looks like a scam, and when a white person tells you, "don't worry about the details of the financing," you'll trust them.

Not only scammers but all kinds of (somewhat) legitimate business organizations regularly hire white people for no reason other than providing a white face and making the business seem more trustworthy. This is especially true in businesses where trust is necessary, such as investment managers and medicine sellers. A white person who has absolutely no knowledge or connection to the business might be hired to sit in a tradeshow booth, or appear in a company video, or attend a meeting (sitting and nodding while the conversation happens in Chinese) -- solely to bring credibility to the venture. There are even "talent agencies" that will provide "white faces" for such needs. The typical profile of such a white person is that they have been fired from or cannot qualify for a job teaching English; usually they are high school graduates or even high school dropouts, with sometimes a criminal record in their home country. Nothing admirable there, other than their white faces.

As more foreigners flock to Shanghai and Beijing, and Chinese people learn that not all white people are childlike and honest (surprise, surprise!), the drawing power of a white face has decreased -- but outside of Shanghai and Beijing, the power is tremendous, and even in Shanghai and Beijing, the power of a white face is something to contend with.

As a funny reversal, a friend of mine from business school -- a white American guy -- has a software startup. He had a potential client visiting from China. He was actually worried about the fact that his current staff has no Asians, and thought that this would make the Chinese client uncomfortable. He wanted to hire me and some other Asian people to do exactly the same thing as the "white faces" in China, but being "yellow faces" in New York -- on the erroneous belief that Chinese people like to do business with Chinese people. I strongly advised him to keep the all-white staff for the meeting with the Chinese clients, and to hide any Asians he might hire before that meeting. Chinese people give a lot more credibility and trust to white people than to fellow Chinese people or to any sorts of Asians. The only times Chinese people may be clustered doing business with other Chinese people is when language limitations or discrimination forces them into it, or when they want to do something immoral or illegal that is considered acceptable in Chinese business (for example, Chinese restaurants in New York hire Chinese waitstaff generally because they are willing to work for below minimum wage, and without exercising any of their legal rights).

So don't be shy about presenting yourself as a white person in China or with Chinese people anywhere. You will not be seen as less trustworthy. You will, however, be seen as much more gullible -- so people inclined in this way are very likely to cheat you. If you are not Chinese but not white, you will be seen as some sort of odd "miscellaneous leftover" category (again, this isn't my opinion, only me relating the typical Chinese person's opinion), not particularly good or bad, but with a general rule of the darker the skin, the less trustworthy the person. And if you're a Chinese American, you'll be considered 100% Chinese, although something of a monger or even a traitor who can't speak his "native language."

You may want to emphasize your whiteness (or the whiteness of the white person you've hired to display their whiteness), by distributing a photo of yourself, giving your business and product a very "Anglo" sounding name, and emphasizing rather than downplaying your status as a foreigner. You're a foreigner to them, and you'll always be one -- own it! It will almost always be beneficial to you.

If you're selling a product to China or catering to Chinese people in the US, don't try to be Chinese or to make your product or service Chinese. Subtly cater to Chinese tastes, but don't make it obvious that you're doing so. I know one Chinese restaurant owner in Hawaii whose restaurant caters almost exclusively to Chinese tourists. It's billed as a steak restaurant. The steaks are entirely cut and prepared to Chinese tastes, and everything, including the appetizers, the tableware, and the drink selection, are crafted to Chinese tastes. But the restaurant has a name only in English, presents the menu in English (with small Chinese translations -- even though it's only the Chinese translations that the customers look at), and the menu prominently features photos of white people cooking in the kitchen (the cooks are indeed white people, though the owner is Chinese) and of white people eating in the restaurant. The Chinese tourists think they're getting something exotic, while they're getting something crafted exactly for their tastes. Of course, this is nothing new. This is exactly how "American Chinese" restaurants in the United States operated since the 19th century: play up exoticism and pretend to be very Chinese, while just serving a stir-fried version of standard American cuisine.

Conclusion

I've told you the insider stories, from the point of view of someone Chinese who has lived in both China and the United States, and has an understanding of both the specific state of Chinese culture today, and the most permanent, enduring aspects of Chinese culture and thinking. My hope from what I've told you is that you have a better understanding, and take what is useful for you. I'm not advocating for you to become Chinese. But I'm showing you how Chinese people do what they do, and how they've been doing it for four thousand years. In all types of commerce, indeed, China has been bringing it for four thousand years -- often with very high human and moral costs, but still, bringing it.

You can consider this book an unauthorized biography of a four-thousand-year-old successful businessperson. No person is perfect, just as no country or culture is perfect. China does excel at some aspects of money and business, and after reading this book, I hope you understand China's methods and thinking deeply from the inside.